D1611886

Our Father, who art
in heaven, hallowed
be thy name; thy
kingdom come; thy
will be done on earth
as it is in heaven. Give
us this day our daily
bread; and forgive us our trespasses as we forgive
those who trespass against us; and lead us not into
temptation, but deliver us from evil. Amen. Our
Father, who art in heaven, hallowed be thy name;
thy kingdom come; thy will be done on earth as it is
in heaven. Give us this day our daily bread; and
forgive us our trespasses as we forgive those who
trespass against us;
and lead us not into
temptation, but
deliver us from evil.
Amen. Our Father,
who art in heaven,
hallowed be thy
name; thy kingdom
come; thy will be done
on earth as it is in
heaven. Give us this
day our daily bread;
and forgive us our
trespasses as we
forgive those who
trespass against us;
and lead us not into
temptation, but
deliver us from evil.

Amen.

Christianae Fidei

God is our refuge and strength,
an ever-present help in trouble.

Psalm 46: 1

Therefore we will not fear, though the earth give way
and the mountains fall into the heart of the sea,

Psalm 46: 2

though its waters roar and foam
and the mountains quake with their surging.

Psalm 46: 3

There is a river whose streams make glad the city of God,
the holy place where the Most High dwells.

Psalm 46: 4

God is within her, she will not fall:
God will help her at break of day.

Psalm 46: 5

Nations are in uproar, kingdoms fall;
he lifts his voice, the earth melts.

Psalm 46: 6

The Lord Almighty is with us:
the God of Jacob is our fortress.

Psalm 46: 7

Come and see what the Lord has done,
the desolations he has brought on the earth.

Psalm 46: 8

He makes wars cease
to the ends of the earth.

Psalm 46: 9

He breaks the bow and shatters the spear;
he burns the shields with fire.

Psalm 46: 9

He says, "Be still, and know that I am God:

Psalm 46: 10

I will be exalted among the nations,
I will be exalted in the earth."

Psalm 46: 10

The Lord Almighty is with us
the God of Jacob is our fortress.

Psalm 46: 11

Speak up for those who cannot speak for themselves;
ensure justice for those being crushed.

Proverbs 31: 8

FAITH

is confidence

in what we hope for

and assurance

about what we do not see.

Hebrews 11:1

Yes, speak up for the poor and helpless,
and see that they get justice.

Proverbs 31: 9

Who can find a virtuous and capable wife?
She is more precious than rubies.

Proverbs 31:10

Her husband can trust her,
and she will greatly enrich his life.

Proverbs 31: 11

She brings him good, not harm,
all the days of her life.

Proverbs 31: 12

She is energetic and strong,
a hard worker.

Proverbs 31: 17

She makes sure her dealings are profitable:
her lamp burns late into the night.

Proverbs 31: 18

She extends a helping hand to the poor
and opens her arms to the needy.

Proverbs 31: 20

She is clothed with strength and dignity,
and she laughs without fear of the future.

Proverbs 31: 25

When she speaks, her words are wise,
and she gives instructions with kindness.

Proverbs 31: 26

She carefully watches everything in her household
and suffers nothing from laziness.

Proverbs 31: 27

Her children stand and bless her.
Her husband praises her:

Proverbs 31: 28

"There are many virtuous and capable women in the world,
but you surpass them all!"

Proverbs 31: 29

Charm is deceptive, and beauty does not last;
but a woman who fears the Lord will be greatly praised.

Proverbs 31: 30

Reward her for all she has done.
Let her deeds publicly declare her praise.

Proverbs 31: 31

Blessed is the one
who does not walk in step with the wicked

Psalm 1: 1

GRACE

for by grace

you have been saved

through faith.

And this is not your own doing;

it is the gift of God,

not a result of works,

so that no one may boast.

Ephesians 2:8-9

or stand in the way that sinners take
or sit in the company of mockers,

Psalm 1: 1

but whose delight is in the law of the Lord,
and who meditates on his law day and night.

Psalm 1: 2

That person is like a tree planted by streams of water,
which yields its fruit in season

Psalm 1: 3

and whose leaf does not wither—
whatever they do prospers.

Psalm 1: 3

Not so the wicked!
They are like chaff that the wind blows away.

Psalm 1: 4

Therefore the wicked will not stand in the judgment,
nor sinners in the assembly of the righteous.

Psalm 1: 5

For the Lord watches over the way of the righteous,
but the way of the wicked leads to destruction.

Psalm 1: 6

Always be full of joy in the Lord. I say it again—rejoice!

Philippians 4: 4

Let everyone see that you are considerate in all you do.
Remember, the Lord is coming soon.

Philippians 4: 5

Don't worry about anything; instead, pray about everything.
Tell God what you need, and thank him for all he has done.

Philippians 4: 6

Then you will experience God's peace, which exceeds anything we can understand.
His peace will guard your hearts and minds as you live in Christ Jesus.

Philippians 4: 7

And now, dear brothers and sisters, one final thing.
Fix your thoughts on what is true, and honorable, and right, and pure,

Philippians 4: 8

and lovely, and admirable.
Think about things that are excellent and worthy of praise.

Philippians 4: 8

Keep putting into practice all you learned and received from me
everything you heard from me and saw me doing.

Philippians 4: 9

Then the God of peace will be with you.

Philippians 4: 9

I thank God, whom I serve, as my ancestors did, with a clear conscience,
as night and day I constantly remember you in my prayers.

2 Timothy 3

For the Spirit God gave us does not make us timid,
but gives us power, love and self-discipline.

2 Timothy 7

JOY

You make known to me

the path of my life;

in your presence

there is fullness of joy;

at your right hand

are pleasures forevermore.

Psalm 16:11

He said to her, "Daughter, your faith has healed you.
Go in peace and be freed from your suffering."

Mark 5: 34

"Don't be afraid; just believe."

Mark 5: 36

But you, Lord, are a shield around me
my glory, the One who lifts my head high.

Psalm 3: 3

I call out to the Lord
and he answers me from his holy mountain.

Psalm 3: 4

I lie down and sleep;
I wake again, because the Lord sustains me.

Psalm 3: 5

From the Lord comes deliverance.
May your blessing be on your people.

Psalm 3: 8

Answer me when I call to you,
my righteous God.

Psalm 4: 1

Give me relief from my distress;
have mercy on me and hear my prayer.

Psalm 4: 1

Therefore, I urge you, brothers and sisters, in view of God's mercy,
to offer your bodies as a living sacrifice,

Romans 12: 1

holy and pleasing to God, this is your true and proper worship.

Romans 12: 1

Do not conform to the pattern of this world,
but be transformed by the renewing of your mind.

Romans 12: 2

Then you will be able to test and approve what God's will is
his good, pleasing and perfect will.

Romans 12: 2

For by the grace given me I say to every one of you:
Do not think of yourself more highly than you ought,

Romans 12: 3

but rather think of yourself with sober judgment, in accordance
with the faith God has distributed to each of you.

Romans 12: 3

For just as each of us has one body with many members,
and these members do not all have the same function,

Romans 12: 4

so in Christ we, though many, form one body,
and each member belongs to all the others.

Romans 12: 5

We have different gifts, according to the grace given to each of us.
If your gift is prophesying, then prophesy in accordance with your faith:

Romans 12: 6

PEACE

And the peace of God,

which surpasses

all understanding,

will guard your hearts

and your minds

in Christ Jesus.

Philippians 4:7

If it is serving, then serve;
If it is teaching, then teach;

Romans 12: 7

If it is to encourage, then give encouragement;
If it is giving, then give generously;

Romans 12: 8

If it is to lead, do it diligently:
If it is to show mercy, do it cheerfully.

Romans 12: 8

Love must be sincere. Hate what is evil: cling to what is good.

Romans 12: 9

Be devoted to one another in love.
Honor one another above yourselves.

Romans 12: 10

Never be lacking in zeal,
but keep your spiritual fervor, serving the Lord.

Romans 12: 11

Be joyful in hope, patient in affliction, faithful in prayer.

Romans 12: 12

Share with the Lord's people who are in need.
Practice hospitality.

Romans 12: 13

Bless those who persecute you:
Bless and do not curse.

Romans 12: 14

Rejoice with those who rejoice;
mourn with those who mourn.

Romans 12: 15

Live in harmony with one another. Do not be proud,
but be willing to associate with people of low position. Do not be conceited.

Romans 12: 16

Do not repay anyone evil for evil.
Be careful to do what is right in the eyes of everyone.

Romans 12: 17

If it is possible, as far as it depends on you,
live at peace with everyone.

Romans 12: 18

Do not take revenge, my dear friends, but leave room for God's wrath,
for it is written: "It is mine to avenge; I will repay," says the Lord.

Romans 12: 19

On the contrary:
"If your enemy is hungry, feed him:

Romans 12: 20

HOPE

For I know the plans
I have for you
declares the Lord
plans to prosper you
and not to harm you
plans to give you
hope and a future

Jeremiah 29:11

if he is thirsty, give him something to drink.
In doing this, you will heap burning coals on his head."

Romans 12: 20

Do not be overcome by evil,
but overcome evil with good.

Romans 12: 21

Therefore I tell you, whatever you ask for in prayer,
believe that you have received it, and it will be yours.

Mark 11: 24

And when you stand praying, if you hold anything against anyone, forgive them,
so that your Father in heaven may forgive you your sins."

Mark 11: 25

The Lord bless you
and keep you:

Numbers 6: 24

the Lord make his face shine on you
and be gracious to you;

Numbers 6: 25

the Lord turn his face toward you
and give you peace."'

Numbers 6: 26

Love is patient, love is kind.
It does not envy, it does not boast, it is not proud.

1 Corinthians 13: 4

It does not dishonor others, it is not self-seeking,
it is not easily angered, it keeps no record of wrongs.

1 Corinthians 13: 5

Love does not delight in evil
but rejoices with the truth.

1 Corinthians 13: 6

It always protects, always trusts,
always hopes, always perseveres.

1 Corinthians 13: 7

And now these three remain: Faith, Hope, and Love.
But the greatest of these is Love.

1 Corinthians 13: 13

Do you not know? Have you not heard?
The Lord is the everlasting God,

Isaiah 40: 28

the Creator of the ends of the earth. He will not grow tired or weary, and his understanding no one can fathom.

Isaiah 40: 28

He gives strength to the weary
and increases the power of the weak.

Isaiah 40: 29

TRUST

in the Lord

with all your heart

and do not lean

on your own understanding.

In all your ways acknowledge Him,

and he will make

straight your paths.

Proverbs 3:5-6

Even youths grow tired and weary,
and young men stumble and fall:

Isaiah 40: 30

but those who hope in the Lord will renew their strength.
They will soar on wings like eagles:

Isaiah 40: 31

They will run and not grow weary,
they will walk and not be faint.

Isaiah 40: 31

Have I not commanded you?
Be strong and courageous.

Joshua 1: 9

Do not be afraid; do not be discouraged,
for the Lord your God will be with you wherever you go."

Joshua 1: 9

For we live by faith, not by sight.

2 Corinthians 5:7

To God belong wisdom and power:
counsel and understanding are His.

Job 12:13

Now faith is confidence in what we hope for
and assurance about what we do not see.

Hebrews 11: 1

*"I have the right to do anything," you say—but not everything is beneficial.
"I have the right to do anything"—but not everything is constructive.*

1 Corinthians 10:23

Therefore do not worry about tomorrow, for tomorrow will worry about itself.
Each day has enough trouble of its own.

Matthew 6:34

You will seek me and find me
when you seek me with all your heart.

Jeremiah 29:13

You are altogether beautiful, my darling;
there is no flaw in you.

Songs 4: 7

With God all things are possible.

Matthew 19:26

Do not seek revenge or bear a grudge against anyone among your people,
but love your neighbor as yourself. I am the Lord.

Leviticus 19:18

Give thanks to the Lord, for he is good.
His love endures forever.

Psalm 136: 1

Give thanks to the God of gods.
His love endures forever.

Psalm 136: 2

Give thanks to the Lord of lords:
His love endures forever.

Psalm 136: 3

BRAVE

Be strong and courageous

do not be afraid

do not be discouraged

for the Lord

your God

will be with you

wherever you go

Joshua 1:9

Made in the USA
Las Vegas, NV
01 June 2023